DEVRET CLARKE

WORK
FINDING THE BEST EMPLOYEES & EMPLOYERS

WORK: FINDING THE BEST EMPLOYEES & EMPLOYERS

WRITTEN
BY:

DEVRET CLARKE

Copyright © 2022 Devret Clarke

All rights reserved

ISBN: 9798848527353
Imprint: Independently published

~ Peace and Blessings ~

"*WORK: FINDING THE BEST EMPLOYEES & EMPLOYERS*". *My official 30-th published book, and my 32st book overall. As I've been working in many companies for the last twenty too twenty-five years, I have seen it all, and have the experience to know how to find the best work, as well as spotting bullshit when you see it. It is very hard to find a good company to work for, and as I am a front line worker, I would like to share some experiences, and tips for the people to relate to, as well as help them to find the best work out there, by following your dreams. For the employers, I know the routine, however, it is time to change, and as you change, take a read on to learn how employees think, for we have not all worked in such place to know.*

Make your best efforts and schedules, while allowing everything to go around you, not you going around your work schedule.

− Devret Clarke -
website:www.devretclarke.ca

DEVRET CLARKE

CHAPTERS

CHAPTER ONE [PAGE 7]
HOW TO FIND THE BEST CAREER WITHOUT BEING A SLAVE?
(THE APPLICATION PROCESS)

CHAPTER TWO [PAGE 20]
HOW TO FIND THE BEST EMPLOYEES
(BEFORE YOU HIRE, AND WHEN TO FIRE)

CHAPTER THREE [PAGE 35]
WORK/LIFE BALANCE

CHAPTER FOUR [PAGE 46]
RESPECT
(IT'S NOT ALL ABOUT THE MONEY)

CHAPTER FIVE [PAGE 52]
WHO FEELS IT KNOWS
(THE FRONT-LINE WORKERS)

CHAPTER SIX [PAGE 65]
NEVER BITE THE HAND THAT FEEDS YOU

CHAPTER SEVEN [PAGE 74]
SECURITY ON THE JOB

CHAPTER EIGHT [PAGE 83]
DO YOU PAY CASH?
(I KNOW MY WORTH)

CHAPTER NINE [PAGE 92]
FORGET THE PERKS, GET RID OF JERKS

CHAPTER TEN [PAGE 103]
EVERYONE IS REPLACEABLE...ARE THEY REALLY?
(WATCH JORDAN, THE MOST VALUABLE PLAYER)

CHAPTER EVENEN [AGE 113]
I QUIT
(OVERWORKED AND UNDERPAID)

CHAPTER TWELVE [PAGE 119]
SELF-EMPLOYED
(THE MOST JOYOUS COMPANY TO WORK)

CHAPTER 1

HOW TO FIND THE BEST CAREER WITHOUT BEING A SLAVE ?
(THE APPLICATION PROCESS)

The first thing when it comes to finding the best career, is finding your passion. Those dreams you had as a kid? No! Those hobbies and interest that you always loved to do, and it has nothing to do with while being a child, nor dreams, for dreams are not of your own. We as adults must put away childish hopes and dreams, for those things are to be left behind you, while you were a kid, but now that you are grown, it is time to open that door of success, and it starts with your passion of pleasure. What you love to do, is what you need to do for a career. By implementing your hobbies/interest into your life, with aim to do such things as a passion, will only be satisfying in the end. Lets be honest, no one likes working for anyone else. It sucks. It's boring, and it a huge waste of time, knowing we all have one life to live, and if you live it in a way while being forced, you will feel annoyed, and disappointed, and even depressed.

Now, as I write this book in truth, I look at my experience as a worker in the workforce. I can relate to anyone out there that went through the worst, as well as experienced the benefits of a good company to work for. Though limited, I can certainly understand every angle to work. Whether it is the worker, or the employer, knowing I've done both. From doing such jobs as general labour, warehouse clerk, forklift driving, supervising, sales, purchasing, advertising, inventory, and eCommerce. I can't forget that I've also done office work, and construction driving heavy machines. I have been through so many companies, that I have the inside scoop. As you continue to read along, you can relate with me, as well as find the information that you have been missing, while trying to find a good employee, as well as for those employees looking to find a great employer.

We are not all blessed to have our own company, and brand. I relate everything to myself first, and take it from there. As I have my own company, my own brand, before having such things, it took me some time to get there, while hoping to find that special gift that was within me, I had to work for companies that I never would have guessed were so terrible, as they are. Names of those companies, I will not mention, however, while working for nearly fifty (50) plus companies, I can certainly know the ins, and outs, and how to maintain. Again, if you do not own your company, you are going to have to work for someone else. Money is something we all need, not matter how much one desires, and no matter how much one already has, money, is something we all want to multiply, and reap the rewards of having money, that can make our wishes come true.

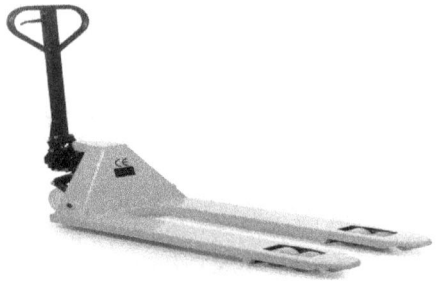

Lets kick this off with the application process. Where do you go to work when you are a newbie? Well, you must first begin in the warehouse, which consist of doing general labour activities. For men, prepare to unload trucks, typically by hand, or by using a pump truck. Though forklifts may be around, you are not going to automatically start on them, so first get familiar with the settings that warehouses have. For females, get used to the consistency of being on the assembly line. Doing repetitive work that will only drain you out slowly. This is the type of work that you truly want to avoid, while upgrading your skills eventually, as you get enough funds to do so, and by going to school, or learning a trade. Before I go further, let me state that, in order for you to do what you want to do, sometimes you have to do what you have to do, in order to get to that destination, while facing many obstacles. Working general labour is one of those things to generate income, and start saving up, with hopes to take care of your bills at most. While you work in a warehouse, your mindset should never be content. Warehouse work is out there, and it is typically a stepping stone to get to where you desire in life. "Doing what you have to do, in order to do what you want to do", as mentioned before. Working in a warehouse will be as your foundation, and a place where you know it is solid. Before things in life go straight, they must first go crooked, yet it is up to you to decide whether you like straight things, or if you're comfortable being crooked, that is totally up to you..

As you apply for a job online, the first thing you want to do is check for reviews. I will touch more on this shortly. You want to make sure the company has a good reputation, instead of a high turn-over rate. Having a company that is always hiring up online, is a company that has a high turnover rate. They will go through workers quickly, and have lots of employees that sift through. If you plan on being full time, hopes are you must stand out, and must understand that being hired full time is unlikely. Avoiding agency work, unless you are new to the country, or just fresh out of High school, without any experience, while looking to gain some. You want to look for companies that have a clean environment. A place where you can have nice clothes on, decent at least, and a place that will not make you have to go through lots of laundry. No one likes to change when they get to work, for that is more time spent in a place that you ultimately do not want to be. Personally, as I used to work in a cookie factory, it was time consuming enough, and then having to change clothes once there. Sweating often due to not liking the size fittings, and such, it was annoying. Having so much employees surrounding, and having lots of ovens around, in a heated temperature, it was never great. What was worse, is finding out how things are made, and I never ate a cook for over five years since working there. I only recently started again, but that was over twenty years ago.

When I step into a company for an interview, I make sure to look around. Not just in the clean offices, but request to see the warehouse. If they refuse, I turn down the job. The reason that they do not want to give you a tour, is due to the fact that it is unorganized, and unclean. Lets face it, people are show-offs, and show off good things, while hiding nasty things. If you have a nice car, you want others to admire it as well, if that is your style. Likewise with your home. Your more proud to show you all that you have acquired throughout your time here on earth. So, why can't they show you the warehouse, or settings/atmosphere in where you would be working?

As an Israelite (Black, Negro, African American), I make sure to look for multi-cultured environments. I would rather work with my own people, than any other nation of people, especially Caucasians. Being of colour, they treat us different, and it is not good feeling, while not being able to relate, nor hang around people that ultimately dislike you. Respect is respect, which is good, however, when people are fake surrounding you, it is not pleasant at all, especially when you eventually catch them watching you for theft, or just backstabbing you.

I tend to look at companies for the hours of operation. Making sure to ask, what are the hours of operation is important, for this is how you schedule your life surrounding it, and I will talk more on this subject in the chapters to come. Co-workers. We need to be able to mesh together, in order for things to feel right. I do not want to be around people when working for this same reason. I would not want to be around people that I dislike for the majority of my day. I can't be fake, and when I can't stand someone, I do not want them around me. Imagine setting up a career of having someone around you for this period of time, and not being able to have any form of peace.

Location, is another thing. For where you are located is important to not have to travel so far. I want to be close to where I work, just to optimize the best time for myself. I can get much more things done surrounding my personal life, and I will likewise, touch on this subject shortly.

The application process is easy. When you finally find all the perks that outweigh the negatives, you are now in the process of sending your resume, obtaining an interview, and obtaining the position. That all was said too fast, so let me slow it down. You must first get noticed by the employer. If you are a newbie the scene, or someone that is experienced but having trouble finding that job, you must do what other job seeker are not doing, and that is by cold-calling. You submit your resume, and obtain the company by searching it up, and then you call them. If you can go the distance, it shows your "want", and "desire", and that is a positive thing. Although it may come off annoying, and pushy, it is still a better step than waiting on the company to call you. Be bold, be brave, and show them that you want it, by budding in line. They can only say, "we are not taking calls", or "sorry, you are not selected". That is all it comes down too, and it can't get any worse. You move unto the next application. Sooner than later, you will eventually be given that shot. I used to sit around waiting, and waiting, and waiting, until I said, "let me pick up the phone and call them". And when I did, I was amazed to get an interview the same day, same week, and even offered the role. It felt good to hear, "you are the first resume", for it shows that I am most hungry, and when it works out, I will not only give my professionalism picture in the companies hiring team, but also give me the perks that I desired.

If you are new to the scene, you may have to accept what is given, until you get the feel, however, when you are not new, you get to further your value. You can sit in that room, while being interview, to show how impressive you can be, by choosing your words correctly. Not to charm nor kiss-ass, but to show how confident you are. I've been given more money just by behaving in such a way. Being able to walk out like I'm worth more than I was worth at that stage in my life.

Once you get over the application stages, continue to show your confidence, and bravery. If one man can, so can you. Think positive, and work hard, for man must work, and show his craft.

Once you accept the wages and the contract, as well as try out any jobs, do not complain nor be upset if other workers make more than you. You should be content for what you agreed upon, and be happy. It will certainly make you feel less hateful towards others, and focus more on your own role. For if you do not, you will only end up sour, and wanting that other employee to match your efforts. Learn from the scriptures.

SCRIPTURE
Matthew 20:1-16
_{King James Version}

1 For the kingdom of heaven is like unto a man that is an householder, which went out early in the morning to hire labourers into his vineyard.
2 And when he had agreed with the labourers for a penny a day, he sent them into his vineyard.
3 And he went out about the third hour, and

saw others standing idle in the marketplace, 4 And said unto them; Go ye also into the vineyard, and whatsoever is right I will give you. And they went their way.
5 Again he went out about the sixth and ninth hour, and did likewise.
6 And about the eleventh hour he went out, and found others standing idle, and saith unto them, Why stand ye here all the day idle?

7 They say unto him, Because no man hath hired us. He saith unto them, Go ye also into the vineyard; and whatsoever is right, that shall ye receive.
8 So when even was come, the lord of the vineyard saith unto his steward, Call the labourers, and give them their hire, beginning from the last unto the first.
9 And when they came that were hired about the eleventh hour, they received every man a penny.
10 But when the first came, they supposed that they should have received more; and they likewise received every man a penny.
11 And when they had received it, they murmured against the goodman of the house,
12 Saying, These last have wrought but one

hour, and thou hast made them equal unto us, which have borne the burden and heat of the day.

13 But he answered one of them, and said, Friend, I do thee no wrong: didst not thou agree with me for a penny?

14 Take that thine is, and go thy way: I will give unto this last, even as unto thee.

15 Is it not lawful for me to do what I will with mine own? Is thine eye evil, because I am good?

16 So the last shall be first, and the first last: for many be called, but few chosen.

To all those who feel like they will not advance their skills to pass the warehouse setting, I encourage you still to advance your skills. The world is moving in technology, and as there are forklifts, you should consider getting as much training as possible, and start working in that field, where you can still make decent money, above minimal wage. This way, you do less work, but is more skilled, and can gain enough experience to take you above the entry level positions.

.

CHAPTER 2

HOW TO FIND THE BEST EMPLOYEES ? (BEFORE YOU HIRE, AND WHEN TO FIRE)

WORK: FINDING THE BEST EMPLOYEES & EMPLOYERS

I want to make this simple and plain, for it is not that hard in finding a good worker. Now, most of the work that I am touching on, and pushing towards, are for warehouse operations, however, it can also assist in any area of work, even construction, and other trades. The first thing I remember a manager meeting me once for an interview, at a carrier company said, "I hired you the moment I shook your hand", and I could automatically relate to him as a man. For most good workers, are going to have a good grip of a hand-shake, as well as, how you look someone in the eye to show respect. That manger and I bonded quite well, and respect was there. When you come in contact with a "real one", someone that is not fake, nor putting on an act, but is real honest, and shows you exactly what it is going to be, that is a good hire. As a man that keeps my word, I never let down that manager, nor allowed him to regret the day hiring me, and I know this just based off of my own personality, and performance. On top of that, being of colour, within a Caucasian company, and him being the same colour as myself, I knew I wouldn't let my people down. Not to be accepted, but to have the opportunities that we deserve. By setting a good example, we help one another grow, and eventually branch off to create our own thing. The thing about a good worker, is confidence, and as I had confidence, knowing I back up all that I say, and always perform at a high rate, having someone with confidence is a major bonus, for he/she will not look for direction often, which is a good thing, knowing you need someone that is not going to ask you every five too ten minutes, "what should I do now?". Instead, that worker will find something to do, and not waste time, for time is something that real workers know best not to waste, knowing we are straight up, and want to earn our paychecks, as well as, perform to get jobs done.

Personally, I'm the type of man that likes to get things done, and stay ahead of the game. I like to make sure that all things are in order, and I have enough room to catch my mistake(s), if any. Money is something that I do not play with, so when I work for any company, I want to make sure that no one is going to ever tell me that I did not earn my paycheck, nor make me feel like I need to do more, when I do the most. That way, I can assure my income coming in, as well as my spot in the company. Not to be a kiss ass, but to be confident in myself, as well as my work ethic. There has never been a company that I've worked for insult me to say that I do not do enough. The only time that has happened is when the company, is trying to use me, and that right there is a sign for company owners/managers to check themselves, for once you do such a thing, you will lose out on a great worker, and look like a total ass-hole. Do not break a bridge that you need help carrying your heavy loads over. It's one thing to have that load of merchandise/material, but without the man power, you have still belongings, that just do not move, which means, no incoming funds, nor source of movement.

Now, as we all know, being employees, it's all about the perks, and the perks are mainly the money, which is the wage per hour, or salary expectations. I get it, you do not want to give out so much at the gate, while not having someone that is sure going to deliver in return. Yet, you must understand that once you have passed the hand-shake process, and confidence while looking you in your eyes, you must give that potential worker, what he/she is asking. Let them have the feeling of "worth". This word "worth" is important. For when we seek work, we want to feel important, and feel like the wage that we expect, is our value that is reasonable. We can all ask for crazy amounts as employees, however, we ask for that which would benefit our lives. So, with that said, give the employees what they desire, and watch how they perform. I assure you that it will benefit you more by doing so, rather than short-payment at the gate, only because that worker will feel as if it's now "just to get by", money, and not feel comfortable at all, nor feel like that role will ever be long term. That worker wants comfort, and without comfort, that worker will continue to look work, hoping to get all the perks that one desires within one place.

Now, I want to touch more on the perks. First off, as an employee who is straight forward as myself, when I was looking, I wanted to find something that will benefit me the most in the majority of areas. We that seek work, are people that do not want a share of your company. We just want work and the money that follows it. We most likely do not want to build your company, but ourselves through your company. We sure do want to have the benefits that benefit our lives most. So, as I have been looking work in my younger years, I've always looked for location first, and then hourly rate, and from there, I look at the amount of people working at that location, as well as work hours. Work/life balance must be there. As we all know there is many companies out there with many different shifts to work, and most desired being the day shift. Personally, I prefer 7:00 AM to 3:30 PM. As I do not take lunch breaks, and want to just work, and go home, where my peace is, and so, I typically just work until 3:00 PM. That shift is the best shift when operating a business, and you desire workers to work for you. I say this, for it give the workers time to have peace of mind for self. The rest of the evening, is there for the worker to relax, heal, and to spend quality time with friends, and family, as well as, work double shifts elsewhere. Being flexible with time starts is important. I'm different from many workers, due to confidence, and as I prefer my time over money, I typically work 3-4 days. I usually go max 4 days, and that is due to having work/life balance. Without work/life balance, it becomes stress, and I would feel more like a slave. You do not want your workers feeling like slaves, and depressed, while doing the same things over, and over again repetitive. A good way to balance this out is by allowing all workers to work 4 days. This way, they can still have time for themselves. I used to hate hearing people complain about long-weekends ending quickly, while they had to wait so long just to get one. Instead, you should create such a time on a weekly basis. Now, this should be an option, however, it will suit your company in the end, and have long-term workers that will be loyal to the company, and that is a positive thing to create for yourself. The best way to even make it better, and more suitable for yourself, and the workers is be loyal to your workers. Those who have been with you the longest, should receive better perks, and first at options. I say that to say this. Give the workers 4 days each, while allowing those with you the longest, the option of working Sunday-through-Wednesday, or Tuesday-through-Friday. Which ever they choose, allow those who you hire, to fill in the blanks, and have the opposite shift. That way, they can all enjoy time with their families, friend, and themselves. Sunday, being the first day of the week, should the first 4 day shift start, and then let it go to Wednesday. Second shift takes over, while meeting the first shift on Tuesday.

SCRIPTURE
Exodus 20:9-11
King James Version

9 Six days shalt thou labour, and do all thy work:
10 But the seventh day is the sabbath of the LORD thy God: in it thou shalt not do any work, thou, nor thy son, nor thy daughter, thy manservant, nor thy maidservant, nor thy cattle, nor thy stranger that is within thy gates:
11 For in six days the LORD made heaven and earth, the sea, and all that in them is, and rested the seventh day: wherefore the LORD blessed the sabbath day, and hallowed it.

You must look at hiring the best workers, and it is not always summed down to skills. It comes down to personality, and how all workers blend/mesh together. I've been working for some companies that have total ass-holes working for them. As they continue to feel like they can't be touched, you need to shake them up. Yes, we all need income, but we all need respect, and need to have a good atmosphere to work in. That is the main thing to look forward to. It's one thing to have a good schedule, but you want the best people working for you. Again, as I've worked for many companies, typically the environment plays a major role for me. From the settings, which is how the outlook looks, and how much lighting, as well as all the dust that I can potentially get sick from, knowing I have allergies. But past all of that, it comes down to who you have working for you. If you have someone that is a total ass-hole, don't expect for your workers to have good lives. That one bad apple, makes it sour for everyone else, and how that person operates, is how your business will operate. Some people think this is okay, for the purpose of having a "bad-ass" to keep everyone else in line, however, that is not the case. We all want to make money, and go to work to have the material things in our lives. We spend most of our time in the workplace, so we want to have a setting that makes us at peace. You got to think about waking up in the morning, would you like it to get up every single day, to go to a place and face a total asshole, as if you are battling them, while just trying to make a living? Going back to the fact of having such a worker that is miserable, and annoying, as well as hard-headed to work with. Each day will surround this negative energy, while everyone else will have to be pending how this individual will kick it off. Think about that for a second. Is that worker going to be disrespectful, and all in his/her emotions, for another adult to have to endure? C'mon, that is not how anyone should have to feel, and believe me when I say, there is so many people working under ass-holes that behave to foolishly, and disrespectful, for decades. How would you feel being around someone that you do not like? How would you feel seeing the same annoying disgusting face every single day? There are some workers that can't get such images out of their head, and tend to stress over such individuals on a daily basis. Imagine having to think about such negative energy while home, and even on days off? Fire them.

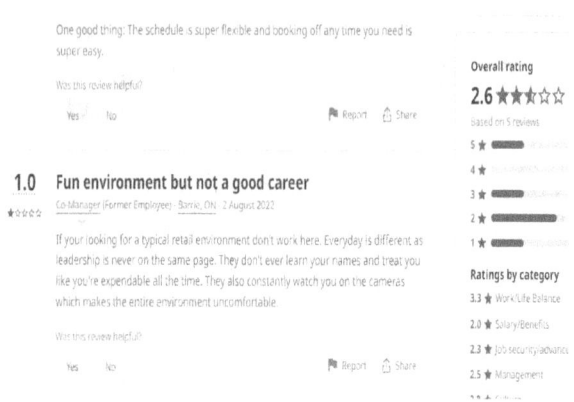

It's time to let that employee go. Again, that person represents your company, and image. Ratings matter. When I search for work, I look at those front-line workers, who take the time to post positive, or negative reviews about your company, and the procedures being done, as well as, how the company/management behave towards workers. I would post them up, but I do not think it would make a difference, knowing you may feel I posted them myself. Instead, go to a hiring site, and search reviews. Better yet, type in your company, and see what past/present employees say about you, and your company. You may just miss out on great employees, and have a reputation that no one likes. I have zipped through companies on the strength of the words of the people. Surely, there will be those who are not even good workers, or could complain over soft things, but the majority rules, and numbers don't always lie.

While sifting through resumes, you should not just base solely off of what it written. For most people lie, just to make their resume look good. I tell you, that hand-shake is more promising than a professional resume. For people quit jobs often, and do not want to tell the truth, due to preventing not getting selected elsewhere. If I were in the position to hire someone, their resume means nothing to me. I want to meet that individual face to face, and shake their hand, as well as get a feel for how "real" they are, and to see if they are sincere people. When interviewing, ask them questions, not only about the role, which will come, however, start off with their personal lifestyles. Allow them to share with you something about themselves that make them comfortable. Get them in the mood to talk to you, and be upfront, while letting down their hair per se. That is a major plus for you. So many workers I've witnessed pretend to be what they are not, and personally, I can't stand it. I want to see how someone is in truth, and reality. See if they are just kissing your ass, or being upfront. See if they will lie to you, and if they do, how do they react when you catch them in the lie. It's better to witness them in a normal day setting, than to put on this image of "perfection", or should I say "acceptance".

Look for words that those individuals tend to use. Something I would ask is, "how to do work in a team environment?", and my answer would be, "I respect everyone, and treat others as I would like to be treated". That right there, is being real, and a response that is necessary in the workplace. You need to be able to have real-ones surround you. If you treat someone with respect, they will not be trouble makers, nor have too much of a high-horse mentality. You want someone that is going to be real with you at all times, while giving you straight up answers, and does not beat around the bush. That person will be better off showing you their personality than to show you "what is normal". To me, the ones that stick out, are the ones that are not trying to impress me, but be honest about themselves. I never wore a suit in my life. To interviews, I dress however, I feel comfortable. For this is me. I do not need to put on a show for anybody. If I put a suit on now, it would only make me feel fake, and that is not my style. Though professional, I could care-less. I'm about business, and my mouth, the words being used, is more important to speak truth, and give comfort in reality, while performing at a high rate.

Touching more on firing people. You need to know that time is more precious than money. You can have tons of workers that are present, yet cause more strife than good. They may just be there doing nothing, while just being there. Fire them. There were companies that I worked for, and needed workers, but hired them without giving them proper instructions, nor a supervisor to watch over them. Instead, they stood around talking, while the workers that were there before, didn't care much, knowing none of us were supervisor to direct them. Especially as the pay was not there, for a title to be established anyways. If I owned the company, I would fire the person who hired those temp workers, and get rid of them for standing around.

I touch more on the elderly that are using seniority over skill. Those who are just hanging around for pension sake. Yes, it is a nice thing to be loyal, but if they do not want to perform, it is best to lay them off. They will get their just due not to far away. Most stick around a company, while doing nothing, and that person is not valuable to your company, nor to the other workers. So, get rid of them. Pay them off for the year, while production will be beneficial to you in the end. Having someone around that can't perform, is a good gesture to show loyalty, but business is business. I feel it would be better to advance the elderly person to a desk job, instead of keeping them on the assembly line, if you wanted to be nice. To think about one, you must think about the others. For everyone deserves to have some form of pros, that accompany the cons.

CHAPTER 3

WORK/LIFE BALANCE

When I was working for companies, I thought about the opportunity to grow for self. You are going to forever be annoyed, and less happy while working for others until you work for yourself. Money is just a portion of it, for that is what typically makes the world go round, and that "world" is the world and life of each individual. How you live your life, and if that amount of salary suits your lifestyles. You do for self. Just as I mentioned a few chapters back, we go into an interview, hoping to get the amount of wages we desire to feel comfortable, knowing it is the amount we know what it will take to make us feel comfortable, and to survive. The key to survival is having it your way, and your way is what it takes to get by each and every day. Time is more precious than money to me, and you will hear often throughout this book. For time is something that you cannot get back, but when you have enough time, that is when time should be valued.

As a writer, I love to give my opinion on real matters, and the reason I write books, is to never get cut off, while sharing this wisdom through the understanding that I've acquired. I like to spread awareness, and to give other people a different outlook on life, and situations. Without time, I would not have this opportunity. So, in order for myself to create such time, I had to work around my personal life, not around the companies that I worked for, and that is important, and what makes the difference. If you work around other people, you will never get what you need done for you, so instead, work around your own schedule, and choose what you know you would need to be happy, and survive. So, as mentioned before, I like the morning shift, and only work roughly 3-4 days. I choose to respect the Sabbath day, and do not work Friday, nor Saturday. I've had it this way since I've gotten into the truth, and have been a steady believer. I keep the laws, statutes, and commandments, and my beliefs are important to me. So, my first rule and set tone that I had for any company, is weekends off. I have not worked a Saturday since, and been able to go through many companies that had no choice but to comply to my demands. Again, it's not to move around the companies time, but my own life, and schedule. I need to invest that time into me, where it counts most.

We all have one life to live, and how we live it, is important to each individual. I look at time, and I do not have much time to waste. I want to be able to be established in the best way possible for my family, and my surroundings, which includes myself. Having something that I can say is my own, is important to me. I want to be able to be established, and proud of myself, and to have family members to not just have someone to look up to, but to have someone established, and in a position to show, "you can do anything that you put your mind to, and you can create your own lane". This is a major for me, even through distraction from ass-holes that take their lives for granted, while messing with ambitious people. As a published author, I may not have made much income through it, but I know that the number count is important, and the quality, for the message is most important. I have already given so much wisdom shared unto others, for they can now use such information to help aid their daily lives, while I touch on many subjects that effect our everyday struggle.

As a music producer as well, I've taken some time away from other work, to establish such a career. Do what you love, not what you are forced to do. And I also go by the saying, "do what you have to do, so that one day, you can do all that you want to do". Though this comes rarely, you may just have to walk by faith, and not by sight, while doing what you want to do, in order to attempt. Being able to attempt is better than "what if". I made it far as a music producer I would say, however, my dreams came to a crash when I came into some problems with some nobodies that took away this goal of mine. It was a living dream, and they were just jealous, and envious people that were selfish without a cause, for there was no gain to them, but destruction for me. Although I still have my production beats, I lost all my contacts, and relationships with people due to this incorrect password situation, making me locked of out my account, while having people trying to access my account. Nonetheless, I have what it takes to prosper, and again, it is better to attempt and fail, than to live on "what if". I say such things, for you need to not come to a stage in your life to feel like all hope is gone, and you missed out of potential opportunities. And so, you should attempt. Whether you fail or not, "what if", will not be acceptable, and it will not exist.

My point to making this chapter is not only for employees, but for business owners, and mangers. I used to work with a guy that was dedicated to his business. Though he worked two jobs, while one being his own company which was up, and coming, he ended up putting business before pleasure all the time. As he kept putting business first, many settings/plans got ruined, and he lost a lot of quality time for his friends, and family. Like being invited to a wedding, and not being able to attend, especially by his closest friend. So, he missed it, and never went due to having to deal with work. Now, the work situation for him got worse, as the world today is basically falling apart, and a lot of problems will occur. Yet, moments that matter and mean something can only come across once in a lifetime. As he missed that wedding, he then missed out on a few more gatherings that would have been memorable, I would assume. Yet, business came first, and he had to deal with the bad end of the stick regardless. Now, I'm not saying that he should have put everything before his work, however, he should have selected such things that only come once in a lifetime. You can't hope for a divorce, and remarriage. You would have to be a terrible person to wish such things. Instead, take the day, and show your support, for it will not only benefit yourself, but the people that are in your life, that shows them, they are worth more than money.

I used to work at many companies and even though they were some great companies out there with many perks, I never felt good inside. It was burning me to feel like a slave, and not a person living the way that I was meant to live, just based off of the skills, and talent that I have within me. There is so much gifts that I am blessed with, that I could have done, and are now just "what ifs". That made me start writing in the first place. This passion for writing took away a lot of stress. While working for companies, there are a lot of people living miserable lives due to work/life balance. You need to be able to have a life, and live. Without living, there is no life. We live, we grow, we get old, and we die. Unfortunately, not all of us get to enjoy the in-between. That "in-between", is the moments that are special, and dear to each individual. Many slave themselves into working 24/7, and destroy their body, and mind. They have nothing to even show unto themselves for they cannot enjoy it. You need to have such times, and moments for yourself, while not feeling rushed, nor feeling like everything surrounds your work.

Again, it comes down to making that room, and time for yourself, not just business, and money. So many people tend to work hard, and long hours, just to live in a big house, and have so much material that they do not even use. That reminds me of my personal home gym. During my stages of working for others, I had no energy nor time to workout, and get in shape. I had to just look at my gym, while admiring it, and hoping for some day to enjoy it. This had to change, and that is one of the reasons why I never joined a gym outside of the home, for it will only be another payment to a place that you cannot enjoy. As mentioned, making time for yourself, and having great substances without having time to enjoy it. You can certainly say, "having a big house makes it all worth it to come home to", however, can you actually say that you are truly happy, knowing you do not get to spend much time in that home, and have to invest lots of money into it, while taking away from life itself?

It reminds me of people that end up getting government jobs. They think that they are set for life, while not being humble. They get this new wage, and begin to fit the lifestyle ahead of its time. No! That is a terrible mistake. You will not be happy, nor beneficial. Most people that I've known that done such things are in debt, and not happy. They have no time for themselves, and have to catch up to paying off debt. That is not a good thing. You should instead, spend the time building up your income, before making such purchases. You need to have that money in hand, before you move in debt, for debt will only make you work longer, and harder, and spend more time than initially calculated, and necessary.

I want to now talk about the reasoning I mentioned in the previous chapter, that time for self in work/life balance is important. I think about those that work 5 days a week.

Those that do such things, only have one day for themselves, depending on the shift time hours as well. This is a message for mainly the managers/owners of companies. When workers work 5 days a week, they basically are working 6 days a week. They get two days off, while using one of those days to prepare for the work week. This is why allowing your workers to work 4 days, is important. Spending that 6th day, is troubling, knowing you have to wash clothes, clean your house, and prepare food (lunch) for the work week. That is just for self. Imaging having kids, and having to prepare them for school, and so on. As those that work have to also do such things. When you plan on going anywhere, you have to plan from Friday, and rush through the days, as the turn around seems much quicker when you are home. When I used to work 5 days, and used the 6th day for preparations, it went by so fast. I think about sleeping in. As I tend to work mornings, I thought most about having a good nights rest to restore, and to build up the energy, necessary to survive, and perform at best. While having to clean, and do laundry the 6th day, which is one of the days off, I would have to wake up early just to beat the rush, while living in a building that had lots of tenants, thinking the same. So, that night of sleeping in, is not an option. Those that work the full 5 days, tend to only get one nights good rest, especially for those who live in a building setting. How draining must that be? The days off, go by so much quicker than days of the work week. As you feel like you are always at work, and that is toxic to the brain. Many people accept this, due to survival, and they do what is necessary to survive. Yet, why should anyone feel such a way?

For employers, wouldn't you want your workers fresh, strong, and ready to take on task in full energy? This can also benefit them by not causing injury to self. Not everyone works at a desk, and those that do heavy lifting, it is draining, and straining. So, work/life balance needs to be there.

CHAPTER 4

RESPECT
(IT'S NOT ALL ABOUT THE MONEY)

Money is one thing, but respect is everything. Paying workers is a good thing, especially when they ask for what they desire, and you give it. Maybe you post it up on your ad, and they attract to it, however, that is one thing. How you treat people is the most important thing. This goes for employers, and employees. I wanted to include the employees in this one, only because respect goes both ways, and needs to be given to the highest paying worker, down to the lowest paid worker. That goes double for the position title. I look at janitors, and think about how they are people that are doing the worst roles in the workplace. They clean the toilets, and that should not be people getting disrespected at all. They are basically cleaning up shit. From blood, to fecal matter, and cold tissues, and even vomit/barf, when someone gets ill. Those who work in such positions are disrespected often, while they are in the worst position to work in. Cleaning up after adults, is never going to be an easy job. Yet, it's a job, and should be respectable.

This goes the same for those working in the worst positions within companies. As much as a dirty job it may be, it is still a job, and necessary to be done. From garbage men, too those who have to get their hands, and feet dirty on a daily basis. They have been making a lot of people feel comfortable. Going back to janitors. If we never had someone to clean warehouse bathrooms, how would they look? If you never paid someone to clean such things as the toilets, and sink, do you know that none of your employees would ever consider doing so? I do not need to paint that picture for you, but yes, I have been in warehouses that have the worst bathrooms, and they do not respect the workplace at all. It's gross, and should never be taken for granted, those that do such work.

For those fortunate to have cleaners, when you go to use the bathroom, do not throw the tissue on the floor, nor dirty it up. Treat that washroom like your home washroom. When you use it, do not leave any foul things behind. Clean it yourself. That shine, and nice smell can be there, if you do your part. Those who step foot in filth, will treat filth the same. We all have done it before, and it is using your foot to flush the toilet. If it is that bad, you know that your workers are not taking care of the washroom.

Now, when it comes to respect verbally, a manger should know how to talk to people. If you are new to such positions, do not put on that "tough-guy" image. It doesn't make you likeable. It makes you hated. Treat people kindly, and it will come back to you. It will also allow workers to defend your name/character, whether you are there or not. Those who have been in the business, should talk with care. We all know that there is many approaches that can happen, and you can take the hardcore route, or the calm route, and in truth, you would most likely say that the one that benefits you the most, is by being harsh, just for workers to respect you, and listen. This is not the best image you want to leave with people. Yes, it will help you get jobs done, however, is that all it is? What worth is it, knowing someone is hoping for your demise, and even death? The saying, "I would rather be feared, than loves", is only used in the streets of gang-banging. Respect goes a long way, and will certainly bring loyalty to you in the long run. I know this, for where ever I work, I move in respect. It is returned, and when someone takes my kindness for weakness, I become firm with them. This is the same tactic you must use when dealing with such tiring people.

When you think about respect, you want to be able to be on a tone level with all. How people speak unto you, as well as how you speak unto people. You want to be able to have a based relationship that gives the workers the comfort to perform, as well as get the jobs done, and likewise, for the workers showing respect unto the employers, they will make sure to get the jobs done on time, and give you the respect treating you like a teammate. Having that level of respect, is where you want to be as an employer, as well as an employee. If you do not have respect, workers will not care. They will walk out the door, when it's busy season, and there is last minute changes. Employers need to rely on the workers, and have that like-minded mind set, with hopes, on hand watches the other.

When it comes to workers working in certain positions, they need to know that respect is a must. Power tripping is toxic and annoying to deal with at all times. No one wants to feel like you are in kindergarten, while having a teacher yell at you, or disrespect you, as if you are less than themselves. It's totally not necessary. Be kind to one another, and talk to all as your equal. A manger or supervisor can still get socked in the face, and have many enemies. You don't want that coming your way. You want to go to work, and leave work in one piece.

DEVRET CLARKE

CHAPTER 5

WHO FEELS IT KNOWS
(THE FRONT-LINE WORKERS)

Now, when you hear of the term "font-line workers", you think about police officers, and firefighters. No! I'm talking about warehouse workers, general labours, janitors, and garbage men. All of which have to do the grunt work, while risking their health, just to get by, and they have the worst pay structure that there is. I can touch on farmers, but I would rather not, knowing I never been in such a field of work, nor studied it.

Lets talk truth. The truth is, most police officers do not do as much work as you would think, They drive around, looking for people to give tickets to, and in most cases, do not stop crime from happening, but instead allow it to happen, and then do something about it. That is backwards. They are here to serve and protect, not to allow injury, and then pursue. I say this harshly, due to having bad situations with the police. Not to say that I am a criminal, nor have a criminal record, because I do not, but when you need them, they do not come, and when they judge you, it is usually wrongfully, and power tripping. They make good salaries, and drive good cars, while cruising the streets. I have not heard too much stories of police doing a lot of work. Likewise , for firemen. Yes, it is a dangerous job to run in buildings with fires, but how often has that happened, for them to earn so much money? They get good wages, and basically are doing more training exercises than actually work. They are typically spotted in the grocery store, shopping, and hanging around the fire-hall. Yet, they get so much credit for doing nothing. When you hear them at rush hour times heading out with the sirens on, it is only for training purpose. There is no fire. They go out at such times to prepare for real fires. Again, how often have you witnessed, or heard of a great fire happening? When it comes down to it, they are not prepared as you would assume. They show up for car crashes, but most are fatal, and/or burned up cars that they take out after the fact. Likewise with houses. I've witness so much houses burnt down, those houses could have be saved in time. It seems no one is there when you truly need them.

As for EMS (paramedics), and nurses, and of course doctors, depending on which type of nurse/doctors, they do deserve their pay, and increase, for they have to deal with a lot of foul things. Dealing with sickness, that may just be contagious is dangerous, and life changing, so they are considered front-line workers to me as well, especially while doing surgery on patients. The thing about it is, not every nurse is a nurse. Not every teacher is a teacher. Not every doctor, is a doctor. Not everyone one in a position is where they are, is what they are, for not every job is the same, even though they all have the same title. Lets look at doctors. There are doctors that do surgery. They are what I consider doctors. There are doctors that are just calling themselves such things, while talking to people. Do not call yourself a doctor, if all you are doing is giving advice. If that were the case, I am a doctor. From now on, call me Doctor Devret, ha-ha. No! Call me a book author. That is what I do. Call me a motivational speaker. Call me what I am, not something that should have that same level of credibility as one that is skilled with steady hands, and patience to deal with life/death situations. Not everyone can stand to look at body parts/organs.

As it comes to front-line workers. I will again,

go back to the back breaking jobs, those have put food on your table, and yes, let me include farmers to an extent, for what I do know. We are those that work in companies that make the boxes that juice goes in. We are those that make the toilet papers that wipes your backside. We are those that put the cookies in the cookie trays, so that it looks nice by the time you open it, to consume it. We are those that have used our hands to moulded shoes into design so that those that purchase such things can have comfort upon their feet, and even high fashion designer shoes. Another reason people should never be so high-minded, for you never know who actually makes your purse, your wallet, your zippers, and used that thread to stitch up that shirt. Those who do not get credit for the long, draining hours sitting, and standing, bending, and crouching, and at times crawling to do what is necessary to build. You will never know what it is like, nor what it takes to go into such things, unless you are in a position to understand it. For who feels it, knows it.

I've worked in all areas of work. From construction, down to general labour in a warehouse, and I've learned so much about simple things, that it humbled my spirit at times. To see the people working in such crazy conditions, and not being respected at all, but being placed in areas that are not only dangerous, but draining, and uncomfortable. Think about the heat. Now, before I go further on that subject, keep that in mind. As we take a quick tour of a typical warehouse/office company within the summer. The chain of positions come from top to bottom. The management/owner, gets to have a private office/desk, which is understanding. The office workers get lots of air conditioning, and lots of snacks, and even fluids to keep them feeling refreshed. As you leave such a setting, you then go into the warehouse. That warehouse has no air conditioning, and has no proper fluid area, where workers can get refreshed. It is typically all that we have brought with us from home. From there, the dust, and filth that workers have to endure. We have to work in sweaty clothing for the duration of the shift, while hoping to get some good oxygen only if the bay doors are open, and worthless fans that blow good air, and only if you are right in front of it, and if you are, you will have sick feelings knowing that you can get sick from the dusts blowing in your nose/lungs. As we cannot move freely to take breaks, as those in the office, and to even talk much, we have to wait until break, because supervisors tend to break up any form of conversation, "back to the slave line". On top of all of that, we get bothered on breaks, as we can't just rest our feet, knowing someone from the office is requiring some kind of material, or something to take away the time for the break, which is not long at all. Once on break, you wait in line to warm up food, and then you sit, and by the time you sit, eat, the bell goes. Back to work you go.

Front-line workers get it the worst, and get the worst pay. For they say that these roles are designed this way, due to those not having much education. Though that may seem logic, I feel that it is backwards. Those making 100k, should be those in warehouses that create the things that we use on a daily bases. Those that work in an office, should make minimal wage, for they are doing less work, and are not harming their existence. Back-pain alone is a major thing for front-line workers. Yet, there are those in the office complaining about uncomfortable chairs. Give me a break. You are sitting down. As I used to work in an office, that role was so easy, and exhausting only because I was doing nothing physical. It was just sitting, getting comfortable, and going home without breaking a sweat. Nothing to it. I look at sweat shops, those that have to work in extreme heat, whether in a sewing factory, or just a basic warehouse. It is nothing comfortable at all. These are the people that should be making good money. It will keep workers working, and production will certainly be up on every level. Turnover will no longer be there, and those working in office, may just want to get down and dirty, to make that good money. Instead, they make living harsh, and reality is, no one wants to work in shitty conditions, while they are not respected, nor giving good funds. They are overworked, and typically forced to work overtime, as most managers would say, "We need to get this job done, so we will have to stay back". That is not a question, it is a demand. I've heard that saying so many times, it only takes away from the job, knowing the respect level is not there, and those working, are pushed beyond limits forcible, for the pleasure of the company. Most companies that do such things would say, that they will give the workers free lunch. Keep your food. I take that as a spit in the face. We want more money. Not to get taxed out and lose.

Speaking of overtime, those who are smart, know not to do so, for the government makes sure to tax you even more. The more you try to earn money, the more you lose out. Which makes you work extra hard, and longer hours, for nothing. It's like a trap, and as the saying goes, "I just got paid, and still am broke", is true to so many people, because all the money that we earn goes to bills/living. You really make nothing, and all is going to keep you poor, or on base level. So when people are jealous of what you do, while living in the same community, they are ignorant/stupid, because you wouldn't be there if you were not close to the same level. Dumb asses.

Just like overtime, there is pagan holidays that the companies will offer, time and a half, if you work on the pagan holidays. I tend to not take them, although I do not believe in them, I use the day off, and rest myself, for it is not worth going in to work for the time. People need to understand that by working time and a half, you are really only going in to work for "half". They are smart with the wording, which is why people think that they are making big money, but are not. They would have gotten time, which is what everyone gets automatically. That is the same amount that you worked regularly for the day. When you go into to work on a pagan holiday, you work the full shift for only half the pay. Think about that for a second, and ask yourself if you would ever work on another pagan holiday again? You went into work to work for half the pay. Example. You make $10/hr. If you were to work an 8 hour shift, you make $80, for the day. But if you were to work on a holiday, you would work, time and a half, which is the $10/hr plus half, which is $5 on top of the $10/hr, and that is $15/hr. If you worked that full shift of 8 hours, you would make $120. Now, you may look at that $120 and think of big money, compared to the $80 you typically make. No! You are getting ripped off, for you are only making $40 extra for the day. Now, that $40, may be lots of money, but everyone that stayed home and enjoyed the day off, made $80 by doing nothing. You went into work, paid for transportation, and only made $40. Basically a full days shift for $40, is not smart at all. Do not get fooled. It is not work the day at all. So many get tricked into this scheme, but you should make double time and a half, which should have been $20/hr + $5 = $25/hr. Making your day of 8 hours, $200, which is a bonus of $120, for the day.

Now, I want to touch on a topic that people get confused with often as well. As I started this chapter off with police officers, and firefighters, not being front-line workers, they may be classified as people with a stable career, however, they are rarely working. Just like plenty of other people that are respected, while claiming to have a job, yet do not earn their paychecks. There are people today working full time hours, yet have not worked a single hour in their lives. I am not talking about the super rich, who work in office. No! I'm talking about certain people that are out there doing nothing, while earning a paycheck. They go to work, and do not perform, but make mistakes, and make work harder for everyone else that has to correct them. It is terrible. There are people that show up to work, that you would not even consider an employee, knowing they are so absent from any form of work. For this same reason, people should never judge any other, while stating who works, from who doesn't when those who usually complain, are the complainers that never get work done.

I've worked in warehouses for quite some time now to witness many men complaining about task at hand, typically Caucasian men. They would run to the office, and complain about a container to be loaded or unloaded, and then they would not realize, that the other front-line workers are holding the weight and getting the jobs done. That complainer shows up, and then pretends to be apart of the solution, and takes all the credit. I've witnessed certain people run to management while the front-line workers emptied trucks in time, while being amazed, and running to allow management that the work is done, while they had nothing to do with it. I hate that. This reminds me of that same situation where I was working in that retail store, and the only Caucasian worker stated to us that he was hired only to watch us for theft. That company that I left, for the same reasons of trust. Truth to the matter is, we are the ones getting the jobs done, while others complain, and pretend to be apart of it all. Yet, most of them get the credit, and we just get more work.

We as front-line workers know what is required of us to get completed. We do what is necessary. We know that we need our daily bread, and never bite the hand that feeds us. We show up to work, and get task done. We are the true survivors that keep this world in order. Without us, people will never understand, for we will always be there.

CHAPTER 6

NEVER BITE THE HAND THAT FEEDS YOU

This chapter is designed for employees, that take advantage of the workplace. I think about a lot of workers that are out there, who are actually not great performers. They are lucky to even have a job, and are allowed to be apart of the team that is holding them up. I can relate this to many things, however, sports seem to to be the best option. If you have a team of twelve within your sport such as basketball. There will always be roughly four to five players that never get to play. They sit on the bench, and they watch the team starters perform daily. As they carry you to victory, you receive the rewards regardless, just for being on the team. Likewise it is so within a company. There are workers that go above and beyond, while they make you look good. They make it look so good, that your work load is nothing to complain about. You should certainly, be grateful. Just like that team in basketball, where they can win championships, and you can be a bench warmer that never played a game all season. You can brag about being on the team, and receiving a ring, however, deep down inside, you know just as much as everyone else knows, that you do not deserve that ring. As you are one to be more of a spectator cheering on the team, instead of supporting them with efforts.

Now, that basketball team has no choice but to give those bench players a championship ring, for they are still on the team. Likewise it is the same for workers that receive a paycheck without performing. You need to push your weight, and earn your paycheck, for if you do not, you will have no say, in raises, nor longevity. If you are going to be there, do what is required of you to do, and give breath of fresh air, for those that hold it up, for when they quit, or leave, you will have no choice in the end, to work harder.

As I touch on a topic of theft, I will certainly share what I've witnessed, yet, do not agree with at all. Employees have a way about companies, and they know just as I do, that the majority is out to use you. The majority is out to make sure you hold your end up, while some take advantage, and others actually give you your paycheck in full. As I've worked in may areas of work, not just warehouse, there are people that I've come across that milk the time. Knowing we worked shift work, they decided to not work as hard, nor care about getting jobs done, as much as making the full shift go by smoothly, and slow. This can also go for employers, knowing they need to hear this. Employees tend to milk the time due to being used. No one likes to be used, and as I wrote a book on being "USED", I can totally understand how these employees may have felt.

They know how you treat them, and by saying that, you do not pay them for the work load, but to get the job done, and then they have no time to gain hours. When you hire people, you should secure the work. I remember working for an agency, and working normal, which is hard work for my pace, and I was promised the work week, but got the job done within the same day. I was told not to come back until they have more work, not realizing it could be done in such a short time frame. I felt foolish not working slower, however, knowing my pace, I would only be lying to myself. Instead of now depending on that full week, I ended up with only a days pay. This is something that employers need to understand, is not fair, especially when they know they found someone that can perform at such a level. I felt robbed of work, and income. Yet, they cared not. So, I certainly understand when employees want to take their time, for everyone needs income, and without getting that full weeks pay, you will have to find other means of obtaining it, which may not come for all.

It's a two way street, and if that two way turns into a single lane, trouble will occur one way or the other. You want to be fair, and give piece work instead of hourly rates. For that is the best way for everyone to be happy. As I started to catch unto this, I began to not work slower but to make smarter choices in selecting work. And this is what I suggest for other people that seek work. Do not commit to work that will end up using you, for your value is important, and without actually allowing it to be respected, you will be taken advantage of. This doesn't mean that you need to use the company as they intended to use you, but instead, work hard always, and keep your value high. By milking the clock, you are actually messing up your own brain, and lifestyle. Instead, find something that gives you the full respect, and value of your work ethic. If you can, get piece work, and do a set amount for a set payment.

Since I've been doing just that, I felt more comfortable working as hard as possible, and pushing myself to even work through breaks, and do the best that I can possibly do. Though these opportunities do not come as often, you can still attempt to try to find them. Employers need to understand how important it is to keep employees happy, and be fair in their dealing to avoid workers milking the clock, and even worse, theft.
I will never mention company names, but yes,

I have known people that have stolen from companies that they work for, as well as the same companies they worked with me in. When it comes to such a thing, it makes me first to repent, to then know that money is what I am being paid to work for within the company. I will not steal for that is against my commandments that my YAH (GOD) has given me.

SCRIPTURE
Exodus 20:15
<small>King James Version</small>

15 Thou shalt not steal.

As I've mentioned, I have witnessed such things, and it has not affected me at all, knowing it is not my company, compared to other workers who may feel they are robbing from them, and it is their own business, when it is not. Yet, it is not my place to tell on who is doing what, for I am not security. I will touch more on security later. Still, workers will steal from companies, if they are not being paid enough. People will steal, just because that is the type of things that they do. Personally, I can't tell you that I've stolen from a company, compared to getting what is just due. If I were to steal from a company, it would be messing up my entire paycheck/income. Instead, quit or tell them to pay you what is owed unto you. There are people that are given such things, as free meals, and they take such things without thinking. Yes, it is free, however, for me, I never ate from a company that even provided food, for I felt like it was a blinded gift to deceive me. It is better to work your wages than to steal, and receive gifts from them.

SCRIPTURE
Exodus 23:8
King James Version

8 And thou shalt take no gift: for the gift blindeth the wise, and perverteth the words of the righteous.

Personally, the amount that I agreed upon is what I will be comfortable receiving when it is time for me to receive my paycheck, that I am comfortable with the correct amount being given in return, matching my records. I do not want to eat their food, nor take anything other than the free water that should be supplied. Others take such things, and are blinded to not realize, this meal will come back to haunt you, and you will be held to do something in return, even if you are not welcoming it. Just like over-time, and working on days off. I've heard company management use such terms to ensure that workers do what is expected, and not expected in return, just as I said, working weekends. They could never tell me anything, for I let it be known that I do not eat while working, nor do I partake in their gatherings. So, I am not held accountable for the return to come my way. I never work overtime, for reasons of being used, and having more taxes taken out.

For employees out there, I encourage you to never steal from a company, for if you get caught, it can be worse for you, and by losing, you can lose out on getting a stable income. Would you like it if the company would rob you of your earnings? It wouldn't sit well with you, and just because that company that you work for, may have a lot of products in stock, it doesn't mean anything is yours to take. Treat others as you would like to be treated, and do unto others as you would like others do unto you.

DEVRET CLARKE

CHAPTER 7

SECURITY ON THE JOB

This is something that I find extremely disrespectful, and one reason that I tend to quit jobs faster than anything over. It is on-site security. The first thing that comes to mind is the fact that the company doesn't trust employees. In no ways, am I suspecting security to be present to help me. They are also used to give directions, but that is where it stops. They are designed, and paid to monitor you. That being said, they tend to be prejudice, and stereotype certain cultures more than any other. Making it harder for people as myself, to work in companies, knowing they are designed to watch us, and judge us, based off of the colour of our skin. It's like needing you, but making you feel like a slave.

I dislike the feeling of having security working at a company, whether in uniform, or working undercover. As I was working retail for quite some time, I had to witness many undercover security that they called, "shrink team". They were designed to just monitor and prevent stealing. As I was working in this company with other workers, they would pretend to be customers, but stand outside the entry of the receiving area, and spy on us. This bothered me so much because the management must know who they are, and their roles. For them to allow such things, that only makes a void in between the company, and I. So, at first I tried to not allow it to bother me, but I had no choice but to remember the code of ethics for self, and if you are not respected, do not give give respect in return. If you know better, do better, and so I quit that company as well.

Another incident where I was working for a company that sold bras. As a man, I would never have intentions of stealing women's underwear. Yet, I would go to my car, and grab a drink, as I disliked bringing things with me into the warehouse. As I was coming in with my drink, there was a co-worker, that wasn't even security, but playing the role of "Ms. Kiss ass of the year". She made sure to come out of the building, and look in the direction of my car, and under the truck that I walked by to see if there was anything under. First thing came to my mind was, "why is she doing it", and "why is she trying to judge me for stealing something I can't move in the streets?". I never can picture a man selling women's bras on the corners. They were Caucasian, and they typically judge every Black (Israelite) person the same. They think that we are all crooks, and all out to steal, while they do not know their own history that is built off theft.

I think about that same shipping courier company that I mentioned in the chapter "HOW TO FIND THE BEST EMPLOYEES?", while talking about how hand-shakes make an employer decide on who to hire. As they had done an external investigation about who was stealing these watches, they made sure to ruin any form of connection of respect that I had for the company. They didn't think about future actions of the employees, before doing such an investigation. Basically, there were high-end watches being stolen, and they blamed it on certain "Blacks", myself being one of them, and though they never came out and said it, they made sure to make it seem like we were the ones doing it, by their words being used. Now, that shift was three hours, of non-stop working. It was a fast paced environment, and again, being a high performer, I made sure to get the job done right, and even got selected into the union quicker than any other worker, as well as had "worker of the month", two straight months in a row. I could care less for those titles, however, what matters most was the recognition that was there, for me to rise in the company, as though I thought. When things are going good, it at times becomes bad due to the actions of one. So, as this company was claiming to be missing watches, they judged the workers, myself being one of them, and for that same reason, I quit that role due to being miss-judged. Without having basic logic, within that three hour work schedule, per evening, there was no time to rest, for we did not get a break at all in that time frame. Not having a car at that time, I used to bring in my bag, and since I didn't trust them, I made sure to put a lock on it, so that no one can look inside of it, only after knowing that someone had went into my bad prior. On top of that, the lock was also there for no one to put any form of material in, planting it on me, just to take the heat off of themselves maybe, who knows? Still, I found rips in my bag to see that someone wanted to really see inside, which is so stupid of them, knowing, none of us got breaks to even go into the room with our belongings, until the end of the three hour shift, and it was filled with all kinds of workers, that would have seen something. How foolish is it for them to not consider such things? Instead, they had their external investigations, and they asked me and all other workers questions, while stating, "just the person I wanted to see", and at first, it blew by me, but after realizing, he suspected it was me, which made this Caucasian investigator come off racist, and judgmental. If it were recorded, as I'm older now, I would have sued the company, just over that remark alone. "Just the guy I wanted to see", to me is, "just the guy I suspected of stealing". Pure ignorance. Now, they had no evidence, and I told him the same, as I've been taught, "I have no need to bite the hand that feeds me, nor do I have to take what is not mine, knowing as my mother told me, all things will come when it is right for me to obtain". After that, he had no more questions, but I had one answer for that company, and it was, "I quit".

Likewise, while working with a high end clothing line company warehouse while doing inventory. They had everyone line up before leaving the company, and swiped the metal detector around us, and we had to open our pockets, our personal belongings, and walk out while being padded down. All of which made me feel like I was in prison, and that was the closest it made me feel to a place that I have never been, but could imagine the process/tolerance that they had to tolerate. Again, knowing my worth, and to know that this uncomfortable feeling, is not what I would want to put myself through, especially after a long working hard day of effort, and dedication. And again, I chose to quit.

Companies need to respect employees, and trust them to do the right thing. If they steal, when they get caught, do the worst possible, if that is what it takes to set the example for the rest of the workers, but not to punish all, nor make all feel uncomfortable, while just wanting to work for their bread. It made the days goes longer as well, for when you want to go home from work, to catch a bus, or beat traffic, you do not want to spend an extra ten too fifteen minutes waiting to leave the building. Notice, you have to punch out before leaving the company, but not before joining a long lime of workers, that have lunch bags, and all sorts of belongings that need to be checked. So, where is that money coming from to pay employees for standing around that time? They should put the swipe-out card machine, after you get checked. Yet, they do not pay you to stand there as it benefits them, to prevent theft. It is unfair. You work unto that specific time, and is forced to punch out. You go to the changing room, and still have to wait for them to search you. Shameful.

Employers need to understand, we have it hard enough working for someone else, and having to put up with a lot of strain, and ignorance, throughout the day. Do not add unto it, by being ignorant, nor hateful towards workers. As fed up as I was, I can assure you that there were many like me, who felt the same. We do not want to feel like criminals, and we do not want to have someone watching us, as if we are going to steal. We will never want to work for you again. And again, personally, the majority of the companies that I worked for, and quit, were due to wrongful accusations, or eyeing me down for theft, all of which things should not exist when you work as hard as I do. I put pride and effort into my work, and do my best possible to make sure everything is completed. It turns me off to know that I'm not being respected on the job.

CHAPTER 8

DO YOU PAY CASH?
(I KNOW MY WORTH)

As I am someone that actually understands how this world turns, I try my best to get mine. As I gear this chapter towards those seeking work, and also give understanding to those that are providers of work, being employers. If you are working for a company, no matter how long, the amount of money that you invest into employment insurance, is a scheme. They want you to pay out of your paycheck, a certain percentage to the government, while it stores these funds, for at any time that you get injured on the job, or you get laid off from the job. That is the only way you get qualified for those benefits that you are paying to the government.

Now, that may be good and all for anything can happen to anyone at any time, and it is important to have such benefits. Yet, how often do you get injured on the job? How often, do you get laid off? Did you acquire enough hours to even benefit from employment insurance? For you must have to make a certain amount of earnings just to qualify. For me, I've only been injured once while working for a employment agency, and getting injured due to another persons actions. Dropping a piece of metal into my skull, while we were assembling shelving units for the company. I had to get a single stitch into my head, however, I was covered for the day. It was a weeks work assignment, and I never worked with this agency before to obtain much hours. So, I ended up getting paid for the day only, but had to come into the agencies office, to finish working for a bit longer after I had visited the doctors. Putting papers together, and them not even considered that I had came from the doctors with the stitch. They made sure to call me, and request I come into the office, and help out there at the agency. Back then, I didn't know procedures, however, I am an honest individual, and could have milked out the situation further, knowing I had to endure infliction/pain. I only ended up getting paid for the one day, and that was it. I missed out on the full weak due to another persons neglect, and lack of experience.

How much did it benefit me for a day's payment? I did the right thing, and that one thing, turned out to never get me work with the agency again, as they ignored me from that point on, making it appear as if it was my own issue. I must say also, that the process it takes for employment insurance to kick in, is nearly three too six months after leaving the company, due to lay off, or injury. Can you believe working for a company and receiving weekly, or by-weekly payments, and then, losing your job, and now having to wait for the same money to kick in? Does rent/mortgage stop due to anything happening to us as an employees? Of course not. Yet, we are people living paycheck to paycheck, and depend on it, so we tend to hide non-major incidents, just to make ends meet. I'm writing this book for the people. The people is who I am. How can one wait long to receive money that is needed right now? This will only make one angry, and upset, especially if you are not even qualified, due to lack of hours. Again, this happened to me.

Now, when you decide to quit a job, your insurance that you invested into the government, is gone. As many years, as many hours that you invested into paying your employment insurance, you do not receive anything if you quit. Imagine if you are working for a company for over two, too five years? Do you know, that all of that money invested into insurance goes nowhere but the government? When you desire to get help, they will reject you, and make you feel like all hope is gone. That chunk amount that they take out is no joke either. When you call in to talk to the government workers, they have attitude, and are disrespectful, while pretending like they are loaning you money. It's such a shame, knowing, the wages that you invested made them have a job to sit around, and wait for people to get rejected, or approved.

With all said and done, I have quit numerous jobs, and I am sure that you have too. This is not because we are lazy people, but because we are people that do not want to tolerate bullshit, nor work for shitty companies that only want to use us. As I've been there, and done that, I openly admit to seeking cash jobs. Working under that table, is smarter in every way, and without understanding this, you will continue to get the bitter end of the stick, or feel like you are trapped in a company, hoping to get fired. Again, if they do not fire the worst worker, who is a trouble maker, what are your chances of getting laid off/terminated? If you steal, you lose your insurance anyways. It is best to work cash, and this should be established everywhere, where companies give you work for the three months probation, tax free, or cash, and you try the job out. If you want to continue cash, then so be it, or if you want to be on books, that should be a choice. Money is yours for task done, not for others to sit behind a desk, and do nothing nut enjoy the cool air from air-conditioners. Likewise with car insurance. You pay so much into it, and am talking $1/3^{rd}$ of your paycheck, and do not ever get it back. That's not fair. Where does that money go? They should give it back when the year is done, especially if you made no accidents. Though I pay my car insurance, this is more reasonable at least, knowing driving is dangerous, when at high speeds, like on a highway is 80-100 km, and being liable, is important.

The system is designed to keep you poor, and dealing with bullshit. I say this, for those who are my audience, are those that are poor, living paycheck to paycheck, and/or just getting by. The lower class, for those are who end up working warehouse work. I try my best to find cash jobs, due to being able to rise up faster.

This world wants us to remain poor, and if we comply to all the rules that are against us, we will never be able to rise up. Working cash is what it should be for all, for you do the work, you get your pay. We pay taxes everywhere else, as we do. We pay to have money stored in a bank. We pay tax money when we buy food, electronics, and many other items. They tax everything, including the tax. When you own a house, you pay property tax. How can you own something and have to pay for tax on what is your own? If you buy the land, why should you have to pay for anything that is your property? Makes no sense, yet it does when you are in the knowing. They want you to stay being slaves to this world, and pay into the best system.

I never felt like I had money until I started working cash for certain companies. Those were the days, when money would be flowing in, and I could see the changes in my life, drastically. It made me feel like I was working for the amount that I wanted. Having more money to pay for necessities without worrying about my bills going over. Paying bills on time in full. It was amazing. This can happen if you work for a company that pays right, even with taxes taken out. For my construction job was a good paying job that made me feel like that weekly payment being made, made me want to work more, and more.

This world is all about being used. Just like my other book by the same title, I already posted up. We must make the rules, and make ourselves happy, while doing what is right. I do not complain when I pay for overly priced items in the store. I do not complain when there is tax on items, and there is insurance in places that I do not agree with, for we should get back some money from investing. When it comes to work, we should all be able to decide how much we should put into insurance, not them taking what they want. What are they doing while we are in the warehouses busting our back, and hurting ourselves, while working in the worst situations/conditions, and having to hide our pain, just to make it through another month. For time doesn't stop, nor do bills. When bills stop, it is a problem, for we must have fell into debt, or we lose what was once ours, or so we supposed. Yet time, is something you can't get back. So, with that said, try not to work for many companies without testing it out first, and seeing how they operate, just to avoid giving out money to a place, that you know you are going to quit, and not qualify for getting that money back. This way will also keep people from doing worse things, such as theft, and fraud.

Code A - Shortage of work (layoff)
Code B - Strike or lockout
Code C - Return to school
Code D - Illness or injury
Code E - Quit
Code F - Maternity
Code G - Retirement
Code H - Work-Sharing
Code J - Apprentice training
Code M - Dismissal
Code N - Leave of absence
Code P - Parental
Code Z - Compassionate care / Family Caregiver
Code K - Other

CHAPTER 09

FORGET THE PERKS, GET RID OF THE JERKS

Everyone will agree with this chapter, just as long as they are not the "jerks" in mention. We all want to do what we need to do, in order to do what we want to do later. Working for people sucks, and as much as we have no choice, until we have some form of skill established on our own, we must comply, and make the best out of what ever we can find. No one wants to go to work in the worst setting/atmosphere, to deal with headaches all day long. As I touched on this topic before, I will go deeper into it, as it is a major subject to speak on.

Now, as stated plenty times before, we are waking up each work day, getting dressed, and looking to make time, in order to get a full paycheck. We all must travel, no matter how far it may be. Travelling is something that we all must do. If you take public transit, as I used to, it is the worst, especially during school seasons, and bus routes that pass many/multiple schools. Having to first wait for the bus, while in a orderly standing fashion, and then, seeing the bus come, completely packed. No room to enter, and when you do see a bus with a few space, these kids decide to lose manners, and morals, while jumping ahead of you, and rushing in the doors, making it hard to get to work. That is just getting to work. And I can also include having to stand, and being bumped into due to over-crowded buses. You may just end up with a seat, however, getting off is a task at hand too, knowing everyone stands blocking the doors. Side note, if I were making buses, I would make them with no seats at all, except for the front of the bus, for the elderly/disable, and strollers. Everyone else should stand up, and have butt rest against the walls of the bus. Anyways, that is how it can go for certain workers that travel by transit. Imagine getting to work, while dealing with all of that, to then have to deal with the biggest egotistical asshole? Imagine having to work under or with someone that is unpleasant to deal with? I had a lot of those unwanted people in my time. They were nothing nice to be around, and it may not have been directed at me, but at their own character, and personality. Many that would swear first thing early mornings, while being frustrated with the job, and may just be saying such things unto themselves, while describing the work. This one guy would just be so fed up, any kind of work that came his way, he would just keep nagging, and saying, "F*BOMB this, and that". All day every day, and it was so draining to hear. I'm not one to swear much, but what you feed your brain/ears, is what will eventually be spoken by yourself. So, having to hear such words, is going to make you feel drained and annoyed. You will not like the fact of you having to adapt to such filthiness of speaking.

Driving excavator

Driving forklifts

There was another time, where this other old Caucasian guy in construction would just be overly extra, trying to be some kind of boss, when he wasn't. This guy was so annoying to deal with, and when I got hired, alongside another individual, he couldn't even introduce himself, which showed me he wasn't shit. So, I payed him no mind. Automatically, he put a mark on himself, as the dislike-able person. From there, him and I would go at it verbally. We communicated through walkies-talkies, and this guy would never speak respectfully, and so automatically, I done the same, just based off the negative energy he was giving me. I had decided to not want to continue working with such trashy people, because you want to work and be a peace with yourself, not at war with people that are ignorant, and annoying to be around. I do not come to make friend, but to make money, nonetheless, however, having someone try to control you, and treat you less than what you deserve, while having to defend yourself always, is not comfortable. This doesn't make you weak, but you can leave in order to find peace.

SCRIPTURE
Psalm 34:14-16
King James Version

14 Depart from evil, and do good; seek peace, and pursue it.

15 The eyes of the LORD are upon the righteous, and his ears are open unto their cry.
16 The face of the LORD is against them that do evil, to cut off the remembrance of them from the earth.

As this ass-hole was in charge to an extent, I had given my notice, and when the manager figured out how come, he quickly asked for me to stay on the job, and actually informed me of the unpleasant ways of that worker. Firing him, and keeping me on the job. This is how it is supposed to be. The worst workers are those who are elderly, trying to power trip, and rely on their seniority. As am sure you as employees, and employers has already heard someone state how much experiences, and how many years is under their belt, while not showing any form of work ethic. These are the ones that are milking the company the most, for they know how hard it is to get fired, unless the company doesn't care to pay out the money necessary for them to rely on. Yet, it is better to fire them, and have peace, rather than having trouble that will make your hiring process more constant, and costly, due to the turnover rates.

Again, having someone who takes time to get to work, travel far maybe, and even deal with the crowds, just to get to work to deal with an ass-hole, is not a good life to live. On top of that, that employee has to leave that company, and take the same transit/route each time going back, facing the same long distance, and so on, and so on, while going home and thinking about how much of a bad day they had. As well as, maybe thinking about how depressed they have become, and how miserable, they have become due to another.

Employers need to understand that by keeping such fools around, you make it harder for the other employees. They will eventually adapt, and also treat other negative, just to avoid any form of friendship, or level of respect. It will become most toxic, when co-workers do not talk at all, but have their space, and remain silent around one another. Trust me, I know, for I've been there. There was a time when I was working for a company that had this Chinese guy trying to be a perfectionist, but came off as someone criticizing all that you are doing. That individual was the so-called supervisor, and would brag about how many years he had, not knowing I had more years, and more experience overall than him, for all he knew was warehouse, when I mastered every angle of the warehouse, from supervising, inventory, order picking, shipping, receiving , assembly line, forklift driving of all trucks/machines, create waybills, and so on, and so on. I have done it all, but do not need to brag. I even took on the learning of excavation, and driving a back-hoe, and front end-loader. I know how to do office work as well. My skills are endless. Regardless, this guy felt like showing off, for to some older workers, they feel like everyone new to the company, is new to working, period, and that is not the case. I have more experience than him, yet humbled myself, knowing he is the "labelled" supervisor. As he was an ass-hole, he wanted everyone to listen to him, while he never helped out, nor did anything. All he would do is follow people, and when he passed someone, tell them how to cut boxes, how to put products on a skid, and trying to school us on ABC's per se. When personally, I am advanced. As him and I eventually got into disagreements, tensions were there, and we just couldn't vibe together, knowing he was aiming to try to take away my shine. I know that is was due to him being old, and easily replaced. They dislike to see new breeds come in, and perform at high rates. That is between him and the company though, that should remain loyal to him, however, he was not working at all, and should understand that the future is the youth, not the elderly. As he would eventually blame me, and a co-worker for the temporary workers that were there, who made mistakes, that were uncontrollable, and away from me, is the same thing that set me off. I ended up telling him off, and then, allowing the manager to know that I would rather do piece work, or work alone. They couldn't meet my demands, and so I quick.

Their loss, for now they have to find someone to comply with the disrespect, while finding a good worker in the process to replace me. It's going to be hard to do so when you lose a good worker, knowing if they are anything like me, they will never stick around to deal with ignorance, nor tolerate bullshit from anyone. If this guy was respectable, and even working, he would be respected as an elder, and that seniority will be more appreciated, however, while not doing anything, and dictating what to do, while going over-board, and extra picky, makes no sense. Those who are in position, should rarely be in position. They should not be in control of other people, if they are not people friendly, and that is a major mistake that they take, while not respecting the other workers, that are capable of speaking with respect and having proper English.

CHAPTER 10

EVERYONE IS REPLACEABLE... BUT ARE THEY REALLY!
(WATCH JORDAN, THE MOST VALUABLE PLAYER)

To all those that think that they can't be replaced, think again. Everyone is replaceable, and everyone will be replaced. However, that may not be entirely true. I think about sports when I think about this chapter. I look at the Chicago Bulls, and look at the era of dominance that they had, while acquiring the best player to play in the NBA. Notice I said, "to play in the NBA", knowing we can't call him the best in the world, knowing he didn't face everyone in the world that did not make it to the NBA, as myself, because all else most likely never got that break, nor took interest. Nonetheless, as he is the best within the NBA, his team got together, and won a lot of championships. Not until he had control, and made the best efforts, while selecting his teammates that would assist those victories.

As they won constantly, they had to do everything that they could do to support the best player in order for them to keep that legacy going. In order for them to keep Jordan happy, they had to pay him. They had to make him comfortable, and also have a good setting to play in, as well, as a good set of guys as teammates. As I've mentioned the "teammates", those are as co-workers, and they play a role in assisting Jordan, being your star player/worker. You can assure the job will be done right, and the day will go by more smoothly, as well as, people establishing your company, just as the name "Chicago Bulls". That name is established today due to Jordan, and his co-workers, being his teammates, and although they do not get mentioned very often, they played a role as well, and deserved to have a bit of that shine. Nonetheless, there is one star that stood out more than the rest. Watch Jordan. For when Jordan feels annoyed, tired, ignored, or disrespected, the star will leave with it's light.

Since Jordan has left the Chicago Bulls, they have not won a single championship, until he returned, bringing again that light, and professionalism. Making his talents be known, and all the skills that he acquired, back into the game. To the point his name alone, brings on much attention, and sales, knowing the reputation that he established, is going to forever be present with the realm of professional basketball. Notice his teammates could not do it without him?

As employers, you need to know when you have a star on your hands. This reminds me of myself, being in a retail company but hired for renovation. As I performed, the job got done well before the time. They recognized my talent, and offered me a new role within the company. As I was young, I accepted it, while not weighing my options, nor getting the best value possible for my work ethics. Still, I performed and made a lot of new records for unloading the trucks with the team that I was working with, and we got praised for such speed, and accuracy. As the company begun to slip from treating me with the ultimate respect that I deserved, and that being them monitoring me, and the group of guys that I worked with, while even using the worst worker to spy on us, for theft. Once I found out, I knew Jordan had to leave the building, for I lost respect for them. As soon as I left the company, all else crumbled, and all the remaining of that team, ended up quitting a few weeks/months later. All of which if I were to see today, minus the snitch, we would all have peaceful words for one another, in mutual respect.

As I worked there for some time, since finding out about this, I decided to quit, and go unto other roles, where I can acquire better money, and skills, and so I went unto a furniture company that had over one-hundred workers. It was a furniture company, and right away, the elders that worked there, labelled me "the franchise". Though they never called me such things to my face, I knew they were talking about me, as they would say, "the franchise is on break", and "the franchise has arrived" to one another, when ever I was there. They didn't want me to know, knowing when you tell someone how good they are, they may take it to the head. Nonetheless, the franchise just meant, the most valuable player. Just like Jordan. As I was the fastest worker, and most consistent, they admired my work ethic, and would constantly watch me shine, as they would talk among themselves, and even eventually to me, about being such a hard worker.

After a couple months, I knew it wasn't the place for me. I quit, knowing they were just using the people, and tampering with the hours being worked. For they would log us out of the shift before we left the building, nor swiped out on our own. Doing all of this to gain for themselves, and once you play with a man's money, the trust is gone, and there will not be any more time given to such a companies.

Companies need to know that great players never stay when things turn sour. You do not need to take away from people who bring gain to your company. Do not overwork such people either, for they will only want to leave. I also have a message for co-workers that do the same. If you think it is funny to take advantage of your best guy, you are going to end up having to do the work more on your own. If you do not take the time to acknowledge greatness, you will only make it worse for yourself in the end. When you have someone good on your team, work alongside them. Just like Scottie Pippin, who made Jordan feel comfortable, knowing he brought his game to the table as well, and performed. Scottie may not have been as good as Jordan, however, he knew his worth as well, and made sure to continue to bring what was necessary to the games. Giving Jordan that comfort to want to stay, and work with him more as well, to the point they are good friends, and have been the most popular duo ever since.

Things to remember for employers, the most valuable worker gets jobs done better when you respect him/her, and leave that individual alone. Giving space, and freedom is important as well. When you pay that worker to make him/her feel comfortable, the longer that employee will stay with your company. By making his/her surroundings better, while hiring the best co-workers that you can find. Although it is your business, that worker is most important to keep happy. For structure, order, and trust can be built, and established that will last a long time.

There were jobs that I've worked for that I actually liked, however, there are people that just made it worse, and it was mainly the management that lacked respect, that made everything go sour. Keep a close eye on those surrounding your star player, for he/she will not always be able to speak on such things. As you have such a star among you, the better his/her time goes within your company, the longevity, your company will be established, and surviving, with hopes to be like the Bulls, and win many championships, while winning time after time.

A reminder to workers/employees. Your day goes by smoothly, only because of the hardest worker, trying his/her best to make sure task get done. Do not lose slack. You must do your part, and make sure to accompany the work of that employee that shines brighter. Never get too comfortable, while that performer keeps doing what is necessary. Doing anything that jeopardizes that star, you will only come off jealous, and forget the main thing, and that is to get jobs done. It's not about who shines brightest, nor who is best, but acknowledging that you are working as a team to get task done. This is a company that you are hired to do your job, so do it right. By doing any form of sabotage, you will not only make it difficult for yourself, the other workers, but the company that is paying you to get right.

This reminds me of a time where I was making everyone's job easier, because I was pushing myself to make sure to get jobs done. Everyone was enjoying the benefits of the rewards, meaning leaving on time, and not having to work as hard, as well as, being able to hear how great the company is doing, while even having the management give bonuses, and free lunches. They did not want to take the time to respect the work ethic, nor contribute, and so, I did what anyone in my position would do, and that is quit. Just to prove a point, of them having to now remember my name, my value, and all that is used to be, while they struggled to replace me. Needing two too three guys to fill in my shoes. Those working in this company, has reached out to me, to tell me how much they miss me, and not me personally, but my work ethic, and how much it made a difference. It was too late for that company, and they missed out. For not everyone is replaceable. You will never know that until your star player/worker walks out on you, and is gone for good.

CHAPTER 11

I QUIT
(OVERWORKED AND UNDERPAID)

Sometimes those that live life, seem to forget that they have one life to live. If you are not comfortable where you are in life, you can change your life, for it is your life to change. No one can tell you that you cannot. You are never going to be stuck in a position that you volunteered to take. When I say, "volunteered", I mean to have a choice to select what you wanted, or the options that were given to you. When it comes to work, no one should ever feel like they are trapped. You must always remember your value, and know that you are a valued person that has something to bring to the table. The moment that you decide to feel like you are less than the company, and they are stringing you along, you will forever be trapped, for it is in your mind. You learned the trade, and should master the craft. Of course age plays a role, when you get older, however, the older you get, is the more you should feel comfortable leaving a job, due to life itself, showing that time is soon up, and you should take advantage of retirement.

I personally, been through nearly or more than

fifty jobs out there. And this number may seem like a lot for many, however, am sure many others have similar numbers, especially those who are ambitious, and want to find better. Though I cannot talk for them, I will talk for me. I know my value, my worth, and all that I bring to the table, due the Most High blessing me with so many gifts/talents. At times it can be a bad thing, only for the fact that I can not be content until I get what I deserve and am treated good. Money needs to be right, and without that, my mind will only think on time being wasted within a company. Yet, as I am also doing the work of spreading the gospel, I have come in contact with many lost sheep of Israel (Blacks, African Americans, Negro), so that is one positive thing I can add unto all the places I've been through. A message was delivered. Still, if I know that I am being overworked, I then, weigh my options, because it is now breaking contract, and sometimes people want you to ignore it, but they tend to ignore your plea for extra income, which is not fair at all.

Again, once you establish your value, you make the rules, and if the company cannot comply, they will only lose out on a great worker. Now, I must say that my value is high, especially within any company that I've worked for. Though they witness this, they still, try to get the bigger end of the stick, per se. They want to use me, and not pay me. If you ask for a set amount, and agree upon the terms, you should be able to fulfill the amount of work required, however, when that number changes on the work-load, you must change original amount of income, or decline it.

We all have three months probation to show what we can do, as well as to get a feel for the place that we are working in. That three months is only to determine how much the money should be and if you are suitable for the role. If you are selected, you can demand what you think that amount should be for the work being done. I've done this so many times, and the company tries to pretend like they have no more money to offer, when in fact, they do. Again, knowing my worth, I make sure I get what I am seeking, or else I quit. It's not easy, but it's that easy. For many others it may be hard to just up and quit, but if you do not, you are accepting a faulty contract, which should never feel biased, nor one way. It should definitely be mutual, and should never be in one direction.

There is many reasons for me to quit a job. Whether it is the money, the environment, the settings, the supervisors, the management, or the owners. The moment I feel disrespected in a way of going against my worth, then I show them that I am not afraid to walk out that door. If you do not, your value will be as nothing, and controllable, by those oppressing you. Instead, walk out, and leave when ever it is not working for you. Time is precious, and just like a relationship, you are never forced to stick with the first person that you dated. The thing about about a date is, there is no commitment, and it is a trial to see if you are a match for the person sitting across from you at that eating table. If not, no hard feelings, move on. This is what work is to me. If I try it out, and it is not to my liking, or for whatever reason, quit, for you can go and find another. If you feel like that first date was hard to come by, then you are in trouble. Likewise when you feel like that one company is the only one in the town. If you live in a town with one company, I suggest you establish your own, and if lack of funds, move, and find something better, or just travel to a further destination. Never feel like one option is all that you have. You can press forward to find something better. You can make your destination everything that you want it to be, if you continue to seek and hope to find.

As a high performance worker, I must admit to quitting a lot of jobs because they are all the same in the end. A setting, an atmosphere, a location, a payment structure, and people. What makes you want to leave the place , is the fact that many owners/managers are all out for the same thing, and that is, "use" the workers, and get their ends up. Yes, the company is important to generate sales, and production, however, without the workers, you have nothing to sell, and ship. So, you must take care of your assets. And if they cannot, the best thing for you to do is, to be self-employed.

CHAPTER 12

SELF-EMPLOYED
(THE MOST JOYOUS COMPANY TO WORK)

I want to close this book off by stating how important it is to create your own happiness, by making sure that you find such happiness within yourself. And so, as a man that knows the value of self, I love myself to know that what is best for me, is working for me. As you can witness the few companies that I have used for example purposes, I have quit. I do not get fired. For I know the value of what I am, is high. Again, not to brag, but to be real, and honest. The only time that I got fired was due to a manager/supervisor being intimidated that I would harm him. This guy was a disrespectful piece of shit. As a forklift driver at the time, he would talk to who ever, however, and that wouldn't play nice with me, so he attempted to rush me to drive the forklift, and once he said such things as, "go-go", I said, "no-no, who the hell are you talking to, for I will....." and the rest I will not state knowing not everything needs to be said. Yet, he got threatened and reported me to the head office, and they decide it was healthy for me not to work there. Not offering me a different position, nor fire the ass-hole for rushing me. Even another employee got fed up after hearing I was terminated, wanted to quit, but left for the day in disgust. Another reason, having to tolerate others, especially those who companies put in "power", is a nuisance, and that is one reason I decided to work for me.

As a book author, I know that books rarely sell, at least for me, knowing I do not promote as I should. Knowing this can change the moment that I do, I have something to offer, and all this that I do for a hobby, and to share, is something that will benefit me some day. This is YAH's (GOD's) work to wake up the lost sheep. Although writing books is an inspiring thing, this is not my only way of financial gain. For as I mentioned, I'm a music producer, and can still jump into that field of work, knowing I still have the beats stored away, never before heard to man. All original and my own. That too, is not my only line of potential income, for I am doing custom patches, and doing moves on the side, while still trying to find other ways to rise up. Am certified to drive the excavator, and it never expires, so that I can always obtain a job, if not dealing with more racist. Don't all that I want to do, feels good, and the time that I invest into it, may not be enough, however, the difference between my own companies/business/products, compared to other people's business, is that I don't mind to put the time invested into my own crafts, even more than I would any company paying me by the hour. I also, do this for fun, which is not paying much, yet I am happy. That one word is what makes the difference, "happy". For happiness will come further when I see my products moving the way that they should.

I have so much product that is ready to be pushed, it is important for me, to have something for the buyer/customer/fan, to have multiple amounts, rather than limited stock. As a writer, this being my 32nd book, and my 30th published book, making me in a good position, for when things take flight. I look at music artist. Some spend so much time making mixtapes, while not being famous as yet. They continue to spit rhymes on records, and have features, and so much collaborations, while trying to make a name for themselves. Each CD, they may sell in the streets (clubs, corners, ext.) for $5, yet they continue to strive while putting as much time into the craft. When that artist is famous, his fans will go back and enjoy all the work that he/she has done, while being amazed. You can even go further, by witnessing "unreleased" music that has never been publicly released. It could be a song that was made in a basement, a long time ago, and people flock to it, for they are fans. Likewise that will come when I become established.

SCRIPTURE
John 9:4
King James Version

4 I must work the works of him that sent me...

You can't expect a worker to work for a company and work for free, for he/she will never do such a thing within a company. I would never work for free, nor be underpaid, while hoping the company takes flight. I find it hard staying the full shift, while working a work week, or should I say, the full work week. Not just because it is boring, but because I know that life is short, and the best form of success starts with your own company, and generated towards yourself.

One day, when I am established while having

enough funds to relax, and take my time writing, making music, or continuously making work opportunities for others, especially family, and friends, I will certainly be at my best, and most happy. It's like living a visionary dream. Remember dreams you have no control of, for you have them while you are sleeping. I'm fully awake, and know that these visions are necessary to be fulfilled. Not only that, but I must also state that I am living for the Creator. All to the majority of all that I am doing, is spreading the gospel, while repenting of my sins. As I continue to push this gospel, through my books, and the craft work that I do, as well as while meeting some decent individuals, I am thankful for having such blessings, and being able to be happy while doing such work for the LORD.

SCRIPTURE
Matthew 11:28-30
King James Version

28 Come unto me, all ye that labour and are heavy laden, and I will give you rest.
29 Take my yoke upon you, and learn of me; for I am meek and lowly in heart: and ye shall find rest unto your souls.

30 For my yoke is easy, and my burden is light.

I encourage you all to think the same way, while trying to get what is best for yourselves. Working for self, doesn't always mean "alone". You can team up with someone that has a similar or even an exact outlook on your goals. If you make it together, you can certainly branch off later if necessary, or create a good friendship along the way.

Working for yourself means, you are in charge, no boss over your head. No one power-tripping, nor trying to control you. You get to set your own hours, and even days on/off. When you work for yourself, you bring your "A" game all the time, for it represents you. Unlike those fakes that lie in interviews, and those who never show their true colours, you are you, and you can be yourself at all times. As I'm one to be the same always, I know it would make me feel even more great to know that I can be as honest, and more cheerful with customers. I can also be upfront more, and tell all those to "kiss-off".

In the end you may witness the results of

winning or losing, for it is not the option, while working for self. It is being able to try, and not live off of "what if?". Live for today. Do not live for any other, for this is your life. Live for the Most High, and do HIS work. Accomplish your wishes, while he directs your steps. You should be confident to know that all what you want, and all that you want to do, is everything that the Most High can support you and your efforts with continuously. Only in truth.

Keep working, and keep surviving.

ALL TRUCKS THAT I HAVE LEARNED TO USE WHILE WORKING. FROM START TILL NOW....

PUMP TRUCK

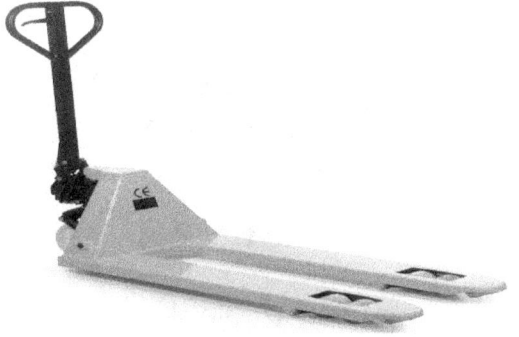

WALKIE-RIDER

COUNTER BALANCE FORKLIFT

RAYMOND REACH FORKLIFT

ORDER PICKER FORKLIFT

DEVRET CLARKE

EXCAVATOR

BACKHOE

FRONT END LOADER

IF ONE MAN CAN,
SO CAN YOU!

BE BLESSED!

DEVRET CLARKE

LIST OF SOURCES

- **The Holy Bible** (King James Version)
- **The Apocrypha** (King James Version)

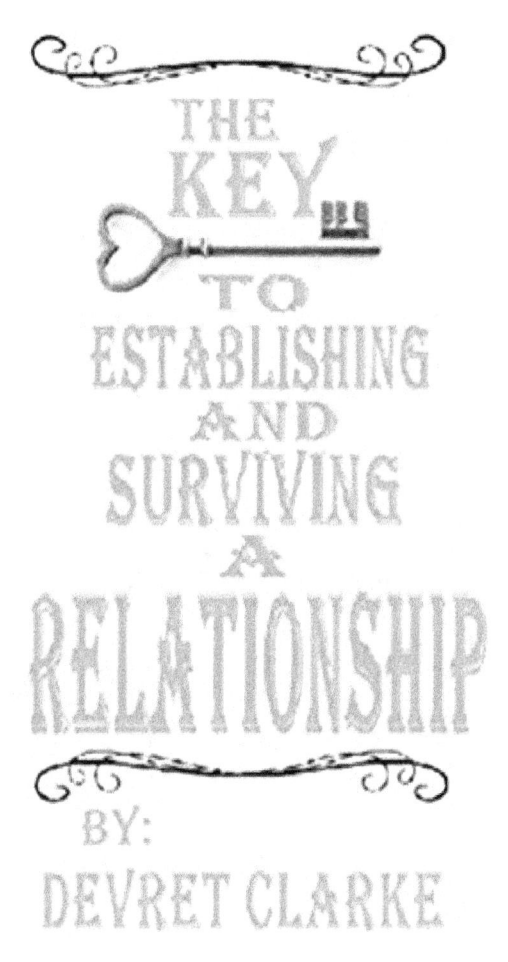

DEVRET CLARKE

USED

DEVRET CLARKE

WORK: FINDING THE BEST EMPLOYEES & EMPLOYERS

WORK: FINDING THE BEST EMPLOYEES & EMPLOYERS

Like what you read?
Support the author. All blessings are appreciated.

https://www.paypal.com/donate?hosted_button_id=TMM43TPRV2VTN

www.ingramcontent.com/pod-product-compliance
Lightning Source LLC
Chambersburg PA
CBHW071405210526
45465CB00001B/266